Snow

Nick Monks

Bluebell Publishing

By the same author

Poetry

By the Canal (Masque Publishing)
Winter Trees
Cities Like Jerusalem
Homes
Narratives
The Love Songs of James Dyer
Gardening

Plays

Le Conquet- (The Refugees)

Short Stories

Aegean Islands

For Amanda, Karl, Saskia

Title Page

Snow- Nick Monks

Nick Monks/ Bluebell Publishing

ISBN- 978-0-9955203-4-9

Published September 2018

Printed by Lulu

www.lulu.com

Contents

18) Snow, Number 3

19) Credo

SNOW

Snow, Number 15

The LGTBI fancy dress party was raucous-

Midnight rambler blazing on full volume.

Normally the kitchen was enough

Finally, I climbed into the deep freezer

And scratched semi happy at the enervated-

Ice in the pitch blackness.

Snow, Number 28

My favourite holiday destinations

Are: the blue ice of Patagonia

The barren Saltfjellet

Cycling holidays in Iceland

Beluga whale spotting in Greenland

Partying in Antarctica

Accidentally wandering into Arctic Russia for months on end

After continuing to walk in Lapparenta, Finland

When relishing an unexpected snow blizzard

Photographing snow in the Himalayas.

Snow, Number 5

If you lose the memory of snow

You will evaporate in anger.

Like a red shawled wood inhabiting ghost

When I was 14 winter bequeathed snow drift

The snow collected and covered brick walls

Undulated along drive ways

The hill was a sledge paradise

During the 14th of January more snow fell

An unexpected windfall

Like the realization of a deep desire,

You weren't ever conscience of

As a functional pragmatic adult

I want snows to obliterate everything

Like fire, an apocalypse, irrefutable newness.

Snow, Number 4

The snow machine is faulty

Vampires, witches, zombies, dragons

Of 1734, 1946, 2025, 2095

Lurk, loom, prowl, drive, park, stand, walk

Just then the iced shoot cleared

And the snow machine created snow shower again

The adorned land was re-covered

We breathed and signed in gladness.

Snow, Number 31

I thought, I acted, I obligated, I complied,

Until like a forlorn injured February petal

I fell into snow.

Snow, Number 12

Imagine if you could say no. No!- to the them

And marry snow.

Snow, Number 10

They say wisely you should run the race

Here covered deeply under the avalanche

I cannot hear what they say

Just the invigorating enchanting sound of creaking.

Snow, a warning

Beware lest the anti- snowman

Melts the ice of the glacier.

Snow, Number 42

I have studied snow for decades

Beware the liberals

Who will castigate you as abjection

Rape your snow wife

Crush your igloos

Make snow legislation

Turn your neighbourhood into law courts

Nursing homes, police stations, assessment centres

Spray coolant onto doctors

Ice cubes defeat lack of food

The snow shall freeze their tanks and court orders

And jam their grenades

We are anti- bureaucratic snow soldiers.

Snow, Number 22

Individually built by the sky

Rained down by the laws of physics

The snow fell into her long black hair

We sat in dank adorned rooms

While the snow- flakes fluttering became.

Sunk Island-Hull

The river Humber stretches

Like a hand of brown mud

On Sunk Island- a remote enclosed bend of the river

The wind buffets you as you are swept into the night

On a barbed- wire fence a barn owl

Makes plumed forays into the field

The first winter flutters of snow falling

Complete the picture indelibly forever.

Bristol, Lower Failand Village

The tramp stands in the churchyard

The bench slats of the night

Across the field flecks of moving white

Are recognized as two badgers

With the snow baubles falling

He retires to the bench welcomes the snow.

Paris

On a bridge across the Seine-

Also along the quay sides-

The November antiques market

As you peruse items

Finally buying- *Let It Bleed* in Russian

And Patti Smith- *Horses* in French

You barley notice the snow lanterns curving meander.

Hampstead Heath

Jogging there from Willesden Green

It's your day off

Leaf's cascade and twirl in random cadence

Meandering along paths

Until on the crest of a hill

You appraise London's skyline

Which is in turn appraised

By first tentative silk crystal snow-flakes.

Snow, Number 16

One room is a store room

One room is a kitchen

One room is where I live and work 99% of the time

One room is a lounge

One room is a bathroom

One space is a hall

There is no covering, roof, shelter

I welcome snow.

Pubs

If you find yourself in one

Text a friend to ring you

On receipt of the call

With urgent concern, say things like-

Oh no, when, that's terrible

Take the glass to the barmaid or man (a nice touch)

Say, I must leave. There's been… (trail off)

Walk North.

Night Snow

It was a night in a specific city. I choose not to name

I was in a hotel room I think

Or it could have been a water lullabied canal barge

Snow serenaded.

Or a semi- detached house with a ragged hedge and broken glass

Snow healed.

I think the city had blocks of tenement flats and offices

They looked pretty inundated by a snow storm.

Icicles hung from fascia boards i seem to remember

The cars had chains on the wheels for grip

I spoke to no one and resided nowhere

But, in the midst of a snow medley

And it snowed and snowed on the city for eternity

Until the triumph of snow at last.

Snow, Number 3

It is coming

Crystalline ice shards are forming

On Shetland and the Outer Hebrides

Scottish mountain streams are freezing over

Snow clouds are swept in off the deep Atlantic

Can you feel it's getting colder.

The NHS, the DVLA, the DWP, the Police, the Inland Revenue,

Are too cold and can't function, they will disintegrate and cease to be

Soon there will be a permanent ice cap over the Cairngorms

The glaciers shall move south

A mile- thick sheet of ice shall engulf Britain

Just like the golden age of 15, 000 BC

And I shall be happy in the snow cave with snow wife

Making a hole in the ice to fish all day long

A new age is dawning and it is called "The Age of Snow"

It shall insidiously engulf this world shall cease.

Credo

And the night was deliciously black

The ocean heaved in turmoil

The stars majestically beautiful, in unimaginable coldness

Together we come to celebrate snow.

www.ingramcontent.com/pod-product-compliance
Lightning Source LLC
LaVergne TN
LVHW072115070426
835510LV00002B/63